MISS IN HER T]

A Farce,
IN TWO ACTS.
BY DAVID GARRICK, ESQ,

CORRECTLY GIVEN,
AS PERFORMED AT THE THEATRES ROYAL.
With Remarks.

NEW-YORK:
Published by CHARLES WILEY, No. 3, Wall-street,
And H. C. CAREY & I. LEA, and M'CARTY & DAVIS,
Philadelphia.
1824.

G. F. Hopkins, printer, 48 Pine-street.

REMARKS.

This Farce, by that exquisite master of theatrical composition, David Garrick, cannot fail to please every beholder:—it evinces both the consummate judgment and the dramatical accuracy of its author, who has here presented the world with one of the chastest and most humourous pieces, according to the rules of art, to be found in the whole circle of the Drama. The characters of *Captain Loveit* and *Miss Biddy*, the hero and heroine, are well drawn, and the manners and language made use of by both, are such as might naturally be expected to arise from persons in a similar situation. As to the three characters *Fribble*, *Flash*, and *Jasper*, they are sufficiently exposed and held up to ridicule; and *Puff*, *Captain Loveit's* man, performs the part assigned him with the keenest foresight.

The parts assigned to *Sir Simon Loveit* and the *Aunt*, in the original, have been judiciously omitted of late years.

DRAMATIS PERSONÆ.

As originally acted, 1747.   *Drury Lane, 1805.*

Sir Simon Loveit	Mr. *Taswell.*	[now omitted.]
Captain Loveit	Mr. *Havard.*	Mr. *Bartley.*
Fribble	Mr. *Garrick.*	Mr. *Russel.*
Flash	Mr. *Woodward.*	Mr. *R. Palmer.*
Puff	Mr. *Yates.*	Mr. *Purser.*
Jasper	Mr. *Blakes.*	Mr. *Fisher.*
Miss Biddy	Mrs. *Green.*	Mrs. *Jordan.*
Aunt	Mrs. *Cross.*	[now omitted.]
Tag	Mrs. *Clive.*	Mrs. *Harlowe.*

MISS IN HER TEENS.

ACT THE FIRST.

SCENE I. A STREET.

Enter Captain Loveit and Puff.

Capt. L. This is the place we were directed to; and now, Puff, if I can get no intelligence of her, what will become of me?

Pu. And me too, sir—You must consider I am a married man, and can't bear fatigue as I have done.—But pray, sir, why did you leave the army so abruptly, and not give me time to fill my knapsack with common necessaries? Half a dozen shirts and your regimentals are my whole cargo.

Capt. L. I was wild to get away; and as soon as I obtained my leave of absence, I thought every moment an age 'till I returned to the place where I first saw this young, charming, innocent, bewitching creature.

Pu. With fifteen thousand pounds for her fortune —Strong motives, I must confess. And now, sir, as you are pleased to say you must depend upon my care and abilities in this affair, I think I have a just right to be acquainted with the particulars of your passion, that I may be the better enabled to serve you.

Capt. L. You shall have 'em.—When I first left the university, which is now seven months since, my father, who loves his money better than his son, and would not settle a farthing upon him—

Pu. Mine did so by me, sir—

Capt. L. Purchased me a pair of colours at my own request; but before I joined the regiment, which was going abroad, I took a ramble into the country with a fellow collegian, to see a relation of his who lived in Berkshire.

Pu. A party of pleasure, I'suppose.

Capt. L. During a short stay there I became acquainted with this young creature; she was just come from the boarding-school, and though she had all the simplicity of her age and the country, yet it was mixed with such sensible vivacity, that I took fire at once.

Pu. I was tinder myself at your age. But pray sir, did you take fire before you knew of her fortune?

Capt. L. Before, upon my honour.

Pu. Folly and constitution. But on, sir.

Capt. L. I was introduced to the family by the name of Rhodophil (for so my companion and I had settled it,) at the end of three weeks I was obliged to attend the call of honour in Flanders.

Pu. Your parting, to be sure, was heart-breaking.

Capt. L. I feel it at this instant.—We vowed eternal constancy, and I promised to take the first opportunity of returning to her: I did so; but we found the house was shut up; and all the information, you know, that we could get from the neighbouring cottage was, that miss and her aunt were removed to town, and lived somewhere near this part of it.

Pu. And now we are got to the place of action, propose your plan of operation.

Capt. L. My father lives but in the next street, so

SCENE I. MISS IN HER TEENS. 7

I must decamp immediately for fear of discoveries; you are not known to be my servant, so make what inquiries you can in the neighbourhood, and I shall wait at the inn for your intelligence.

Pu. I'll patrole hereabouts, and examine all that pass; but I've forgot the word, sir—miss Biddy—

Capt. L. Bellair.

Pu. A young lady of wit, beauty, and fifteen thousand pounds fortune——But, sir——

Capt. L. What do you say, Puff?

Pu. If your honour pleases to consider that I had a wife in town, whom I left somewhat abruptly half a year ago, you'll think it, I believe, but decent to make some inquiry after her first: to be sure, it would be some small consolation to me to know whether the poor woman is living, or has made away with herself, or——

Capt. L. Pr'ythee, don't distract me; a moment's delay is of the utmost consequence; I must insist upon an immediate compliance with my commands. [*exit.*

Pu. The devil's in these fiery young fellows; they think of nobody's wants but their own. He does not consider that I am flesh and blood as well as himself. However, I may kill two birds at once; for I shan't be surprised if I meet my lady walking the streets.—But who have we here? Sure I should know that face.

Enter Jasper, from a house.

Who's that? My old acquaintance, Jasper?

Jas. What, Puff! are you here?

Pu. My dear friend! Well, and now Jasper, still easy and happy! Toujours le même!—What intrigues now? What girls have you ruined, and what cuckolds made, since you and I beat up together, eh?

G

Jas. Faith, business hath been very brisk during the war; men are scarce, you know; not that I can say I ever wanted amusement in the worst of times. But harkye, Puff——

Pu. Not a word aloud, I am incognito.

Jas. Why, faith, I should not have known you, if you had not spoke first; you seem to be a little en dishabille too, as well as incognito. Whom do you honour with your service now? Are you from the wars?

Pu. Piping hot, I assure you; fire and smoke will tarnish; a man that will go into such service as I have been, will find his clothes the worse for wear, take my word for it: But how is it with you, friend Jasper? What, you still serve, I see? You live at that house, I suppose?

Jas. I don't absolutely live, but I am most of my time there; I have within these two months entered into the service of an old gentleman, who hired a reputable servant, and dressed him as you see, because he has taken it into his head to fall in love.

Pu. False appetite and second childhood! But pr'ythee, what's the object of his passion?

Jas. No less than a virgin of sixteen, I assure you.

Pu. Oh, the toothless old dotard!

Jas. And he mumbles, and plays with her till his mouth waters; and then he chuckles till he cries, and calls it his Bid and his Bidsy, and is so foolishly fond.

Pu. Bidsy! what's that?——

Jas. Her name is Biddy.

Pu. Biddy! What, miss Biddy Bellair?

Jas. The same.

Pu. I have no luck, to be sure.. (*aside*)—Oh! I have heard of her; she's of a pretty good family,

SCENE I.   MISS IN HER TEENS.   9

and has some fortune, I know. But are things settled? Is the marriage fixed?

Jas. Not absolutely; the girl, I believe, detests him; but her aunt, a very good, prudent old lady, has given her consent, if he can gain her niece's; how it will end I can't tell——but I am hot upon't myself.

Pu. The devil! not marriage, I hope.

Jas. That is not yet determined.

Pu. Who is the lady, pray?

Jas. A maid in the same family, a woman of honour, I assure you: she has one husband already, a scoundrel sort of a fellow, that has run away from her, and listed for a soldier; so, towards the end of the campaign, she hopes to have a certificate he's knocked 'o'th head; if not, I suppose we shall settle matters another way.

Pu. Well, speed the plough. But, harkye, consummate without the certificate, if you can, keep your neck out of the collar—do—I have wore it these two years, and damnably galled I am.

Jas. I'll take your advice; but I must run away to my master, who will be impatient for an answer to his message, which I have just delivered to the young lady; so, dear Mr. Puff, I am your most obedient humble servant.

Pu. And I must to our agent's for my arrears. If you have an hour to spare, you'll hear of me at George's, or the Tilt-yard.—Au revoir, as we say abroad. [*exit Jasper.*] Thus we are as civil and as false as our betters. Jasper and I were always the beau monde exactly: we ever hated one another heartily, yet always shake hands. But now to my master, with a head full of news and a heart full of joy.   (*going, starts.*)

Angels and ministers of grace, defend me!

It can't be! By heav'ns, it is that fretful porcupine, my wife! I can't stand it; what shall I do? I'll try to avoid her.

Enter Tag.

Tag. It must be he! I'll swear to the rogue at a mile's distance; he either has not seen me, or won't know me: if I can keep my temper, I'll try him further. Pray, good sir, if I may be so bold—

Pu. I have nothing for you, good woman; don't trouble me.

Tag. If your honour pleases to look this way—

Pu. The kingdom is over-run with beggars; I suppose the last I gave to has sent this; but I have no more loose silver about me, so, pr'ythee, woman, don't disturb me.

Tag. I can hold out no longer: oh, you villain, you! Where have you been, scoundrel? Do you know me now, varlet? (*seizes him.*

Pu. Here, watch, watch! zounds, I shall have my pocket picked.

Tag. Own me this minute, hang-dog, and confess every thing, or, by the rage of an injured woman, I'll raise up the neighbourhood, throttle you, and send you to Newgate.

Pu. Amazement! what, my own dear Tag! Come to my arms, and let me press you to my heart, that pants for thee, and only thee, my true and lawful wife.—Now, my stars have overpaid me for the fatigue and danger of the field; I have wandered about like Achilles in search of faithful Penelope, and the gods have brought me to this happy spot.

(*embraces her.*

Tag. The fellow's crack'd for certain! Leave your bombastic stuff, and tell me, rascal, why you left me, and where you have been these six months, eh?

Pu. We'll reserve my adventures for our happy winter's evenings—I shall only tell you now, that my heart beat so strong in my country's cause, and being instigated by either honour or the devil, (I can't tell which), I set out for Flanders, to gather laurels, and lay 'em at thy feet.

Tag. You left me to starve, villain, and beg my bread, you did so.

Pu. I left you too hastily, I must confess, and often has my conscience stung me for it.—I am got into an officer's service, have been in several actions, gained some credit by my behaviour, and am now returned with my master to indulge the genteeler passions.

Tag. Don't think to fob me off with this nonsensical talk; what have you brought me home besides?

Pu. Honour and immoderate love.

Tag. I could tear your eyes out.

Pu. Temperance, or I walk off.

Tag. Temperance, traitor, temperance! What can you say for yourself? Leave me to the wide world—

Pu. Well, I have been in the wide world too, han't I? What would the woman have?

Tag. Reduce me to the necessity of going to service. *(cries.*

Pu. Why I'm in service too, your lord and master, an't I, you saucy jade you?—Come, where dost live, hereabouts? Hast got good vails? Dost go to market? Come, give me a kiss, darling, and tell me where I shall pay my duty to thee.

Tag. Why there I live, at that house.

(pointing to the house Jasper came out of.

Pu. What, there! that house?

Tag. Yes, there, that house.—

Pu. Huzza! We're made for ever, you slut you! Huzza! Every thing conspires this day to make me happy—Prepare for an inundation of joy! My master is in love with your miss Biddy over head and ears, and she with him: I know she is courted by some old fool, and her aunt is not against the match; but now we are come, the town will be relieved, and the governor brought over; in plain English, our fortune is made; my master must marry the lady, and the old gentleman may go to the devil.

Tag. Hey-day! What's all this?

Pu. Say no more, the dice are thrown, doublets for us; away to your young mistress, while I run to my master; tell her—Rhodophil! Rhodophil! will be with her immediately; then if her blood does not mount to her face like quick-silver in a weather-glass, and point to extreme hot, believe the whole to be a lie, and your husband no politician.

Tag. This is news indeed! I have had the place but a little while, and have not quite got into the secrets of the family; but part of your story is true, and if you bring your master, and miss is willing, I warrant we'll be too hard for the old folks.

Pu. I'll about it straight!—but hold, Tag, I had forgot—Pray, how does Mr. Jasper do?

Tag. Mr. Jasper!—What do you mean? I—I—I—

Pu. What, out of countenance, child; oh, fie! Speak plain, my dear—and the certificate, when comes that, eh, love?

Tag. He has sold himself and turned conjurer, or he would never have known it. *(aside.*

Pu. Are not you a jade? Are you not a Jezabel?— Ar'nt you a—

Tag. O ho, temperance, or I walk off—

Pu. I know I am not finished yet, and so I am

easy; but more thanks to my fortune than your virtue, madam.

Tag. Away to your master, I'll prepare his reception within.

Pu. Shall I bring the certificate with me? [*exit.*

Tag. Go, you graceless rogue, you richly deserve it. [*exit.*

SCENE II. A CHAMBER.

Enter Biddy.

Bid. How unfortunate a poor girl am I! dare not tell my secret to any body, and if I don't I'm undone —Heigho! (*sighs.*

Enter Tag.

Pray, Tag, is my aunt gone to her lawyer about me? Heigho!

Tag. What's that sigh for, my dear young mistress?

Bid. I did not sigh, not I— (*sighs.*

Tag. Nay, never gulp 'em down, they are the worst things you can swallow. There's something in that little heart of yours, that swells it and puffs it, and will burst it at last, if you don't give it vent.

Bid. What would you have me tell you? (*sighs.*

Tag. Come, come, you are afraid I'll betray you, but you had as good speak; I may do you some service you little think of.

Bid. It is not in your power, Tag, to give me what I want. (*sighs.*

Tag. Not directly, perhaps; but I may be the means of helping you to it; as, for example—If you should not like to marry the old man your aunt designs for you, one may find a way to break—

Bid. His neck, Tag.

Tag. Or the match; either will do, child.

Bid. I don't care which indeed, so I was clear of him—I don't think I'm fit to be married.

Tag. To him, you mean—you have no objection to marriage, but the man, and I applaud you for it: But come, courage, miss, never keep it in; out with it all—

Bid. If you'll ask me any questions, I'll answer 'em; but I can't tell you any thing of myself, I shall blush if I do.

Tag. Well then—In the first place, pray tell me, miss Biddy Bellair, if you don't like somebody better than old sir Simon Loveit?

Bid. Heigho!

Tag. What's heigho, miss?

Bid. When I say heigho! it means, yes.

Tag. Very well; and this somebody is a young handsome fellow?

Bid. Heigho!

Tag. And if you were once his, you would be as merry as the best of us?

Bid. Heigho!

Tag. So far so good; and since I have got you to wet your feet, souse over head at once, and the pain will be over.

Bid. There—then (*a long sigh.*) Now help me out, Tag, as fast as you can.

Tag. When did you hear from your gallant?

Bid. Never, since he went to the army.

Tag. How so?

Bid. I was afraid the letters would fall into my aunt's hands, so I would not let him write to me; but I had a better reason then.

Tag. Pray, let's hear that too.

Bid. Why, I thought if I should write to him and promise him to love nobody else, and should afterwards change my mind, he might think I was inconstant, and call me a coquette.

Tag. What a simple innocent it is! *(aside)* And have you changed your mind, miss?

Bid. No indeed, Tag, I love him the best of any of 'em.

Tag. Of any of 'em! Why, have you any more?

Bid. Pray, don't ask me.

Tag. Nay, miss, if you only trust me by halves, you can't expect—

Bid. I will trust you with every thing.—When I parted with him, I grew melancholy; so, in order to divert me, I have let two others court me till he returns again.

Tag. Is that all, my dear? Mighty simple, indeed.
(aside.

Bid. One of 'em is a fine blustering man, and is called captain Flash; he's always talking of fighting and wars; he thinks he's sure of me, but I shall baulk him: we shall see him this afternoon, for he pressed strongly to come, and I have given him leave, while my aunt's taking her afternoon's nap.

Tag. And who is the other, pray?

Bid. Quite another sort of man; he speaks like a lady for all the world, and never swears, as Mr. Flash does, but wears nice white gloves, and tells me what ribands become my complexion, where to stick my patches, who is the best milliner, where they sell the best tea, and which is the best wash for the face and the best paste for the hands; he is always playing with my fan, and showing his teeth; and whenever I speak, he pats me—so—and cries.—The devil take me, miss Biddy, but you'll be my perdition——Ha, ha, ha!

Tag. Oh, the pretty creature! and what do you call him, pray?

Bid. His name is Fribble, and you shall see him too; for by mistake I appointed them at the same time; but you must help me out with 'em,

Tag. And suppose your favourite should come too?

Bid. I should not care what became of the others.

Tag. What's his name?

Bid. It begins with an R—h—o—

Tag. I'll be hanged if it is not Rhodophil.

Bid. I am frightened at you! You are a witch.

Tag. I am so, and can tell your fortune too. Look me in the face. The gentleman you love most in the world will be at our house this afternoon; he arrived from the army this morning, and dies till he sees you.

Bid. Is he come, Tag? don't joke with me—

Tag. Not to keep you longer in suspence, you must know, the servant of your Strephon, by some unaccountable fate or other, is my lord and master; he has just been with me, and told me of his master's arrival and impatience—

Bid. Oh, my dear, dear Tag, you have put me out of my wits—I am all over in a flutter. I shall leap out of my skin—I don't know what to do with myself—Is he come, Tag?—I am ready to faint—I'd give the word I had put on another dress to-day.

Tag. I assure you, miss, you look charmingly!

Bid. Do I indeed, though? I'll alter my hair immediately.

Tag. We'll go to dinner first, and then I'll assist you.

Bid. Dinner! I can't eat a morsel—I don't know what's the matter with me—my ears tingle, my heart beats, my face flushes, and I tremble every joint of me—I must run in and look at myself in the glass this moment.— [*exit.*

SCENE I.   MISS IN HER TEENS.   17

Tag. Yes, she has it, and deeply too; this is no hypocrisy—
Not art but nature now performs her part,
And every word's the language of the heart. [*exit.*

ACT THE SECOND.

SCENE I. THE SAME.

Enter Captain Loveit, Biddy, Tag, and Puff.

Capt. L. To find you still constant, and to arrive at such a critical juncture, is the height of fortune and happiness.

Bid. Nothing shall force me from you; and if I am secure of your affections—

Pu. I'll be bound for him, madam, and give you any security you can ask.

Tag. Every thing goes on to our wish, sir; I just now had a second conference with my old lady, and she was so convinced by my arguments, that she returned instantly to the lawyer to forbid the drawing out of any writings at all, and she is determined never to thwart miss's inclinations, and left it to us to give the old gentleman his discharge at the next visit.

Capt. L. Shall I undertake the old dragon?

Tag. If we have occasion for help, we shall call for you.

Bid. I expect him every moment, therefore I'll tell you what, Rhodophil, you and your man shall be locked up in my bed-chamber till we have settled matters with the old gentleman.

Capt. L. Do what you please with me.

Bid. You must not be impatient, though.

Capt. L. I can undergo any thing with such a re

ward in view; one kiss and I'll be quite resigned—And now show me the way. [*exeunt.*

Tag. Come, sirrah, when I have got you under lock and key I shall bring you to reason.

Pu. Are your wedding-clothes ready, my dove? The certificate's come.

Tag. Go follow your captain, sirrah—March—You may thank heaven I had patience to stay so long. [*exit, with Puff.*

Re-enter Biddy.

Bid. I was very much alarmed for fear my two gallants should come in upon us unawares; we should have had sad work if they had; I find I love Rhodophil vastly, for, though my other sparks flatter me more, I can't abide the thoughts of 'em now—I have business upon my hands enough to turn my little head; but, 'egad, my heart's good, and a fig for dangers—Let me see, what shall I do with my two gallants? I must at least, part with 'em decently. Suppose I set 'em together by the ears? The luckiest thought in the world! for, if they won't quarrel (as I believe they won't) I can break with them for cowards, and very justly dismiss 'em my service; and if they will fight, and one of them should be killed, the other will certainly be hanged or run away; and so I shall very handsomely get rid of both.

Re-enter Tag.

Well Tag, are they safe?

Tag. I think so; the door's double locked, and I have the key in my pocket.

Bid. That's pure; but have you given them any thing to divert 'em?

Tag. I have given the captain one of your old gloves to mumble; but my Strephon is diverting himself with the more substantial comforts of a cold venison pastry.

SCENE I.   MISS IN HER TEENS.   19

Bid. What shall we do with the next that comes?

Tag. If Mr. Fribble comes first, I'll clap him up into my lady's store-room; I suppose he is a great maker of marmalade himself, and will have an opportunity of making some critical remarks upon our pastry and sweatmeats.

Bid. When one of 'em comes, do you go and watch for the other, and as soon as you see him, run in to us and pretend it is my aunt, and so we shall have an excuse to lock him up till we want him.

Tag. You may depend upon me.—Here is one of 'em—

Enter Fribble.

Bid. Mr. Fribble, your servant—

Frib. Miss Biddy, your slave—I hope I have not come upon you abruptly; I should have waited upon you sooner, but an accident happened that discomposed me so, that I was obliged to go home again to take drops.

Bid. Indeed you don't look well, sir.—Go, Tag, and do as I bid you.

Tag. I will, madam.   [*exit.*

Bid. I have set my maid to watch my aunt, that we mayn't be surprised by her.

Frib. Your prudence is equal to your beauty, miss; and I hope your permitting me to kiss your hands, will be no impeachment to your understanding.

Bid. I hate the sight of him. (*aside*)—I was afraid I should not have had the pleasure of seeing you; pray let me know what accident you met with, and what's the matter with your hand. I shan't be easy till I know.

Frib. Well, I vow, Miss Biddy, you're a good creeter—I'll endeavour to muster up what little spirits I have and tell you the whole affair—Hem!—But first you must give me leave to make you a present of a small pot of my lip-salve: my servant made it this morning; the ingredients are innocent, I assure you; nothing but the best virgin-wax, conserve of roses, and lily of the valley water.

Bid. I thank you, sir; but my lips are generally red, and when they an't I bite 'em.

Frib. I bite my own sometimes, to pout 'em a little; but this will give them a softness, colour, and an agreeable moister—Thus let me make an humble offering at that shrine where I have already sacrificed my heart. *(kneels and gives the lip-salve.*

Bid. Upon my word, that's very prettily expressed; you are positively the best company in the world—I wish he was out of the house *(aside.*

Frib. But to return to my accident, and the reason why my hand is in this condition—I beg you'll excuse the appearance of it, and be satisfied that nothing but mere necessity could have forced me to appear thus muffled before you.

Bid. I am very willing to excuse any misfortune that happens to you, sir. *(courtesies.*

Frib. You are vastly good indeed—Thus it was—Hem!—You must know, miss, there is not an animal in the creation I have so great an aversion to, as those hackney-coach fellows—As I was coming out of my lodgings, says one of 'em to me,—" Would your honour have a coach?"—" No, man," said I, " not now," with all the civility imaginable.—" I'll carry you and your doll too," said he, " Miss Margery, for the same price."—Upon which the masculine beasts about us fell a laughing; then I turned round in a great passion, " Curse me," says I, " fellow, but I'll trounce thee."—And as I was holding out my hand in a threatening poster—thus—he makes a cut at me with his whip, and striking me over the nail of my finger, it gave me such exquisite

SCENE I.   MISS IN HER TEENS.   21

torter that I fainted away; and while I was in this condition, the mob picked my pocket of my purse, my scissars, my Mecca smelling-bottle, and my huswife.

Bid. I shall laugh in his face. (*aside*)—I am afraid you are in great pain; pray sit down, Mr. Fribble; but I hope your hand is in no danger? (*they sit.*)

Frib. Not in the least, ma'am; pray don't be apprehensive—A milk poultice, and a gentle sudorific to-night, with a little manna in the morning, I am confident will relieve me entirely.

Bid. But pray, Mr. Fribble, do you make use of a huswife?

Frib. I can't do without it, ma'am; there is a club of us, all young bachelors, the sweetest society in the world; and we meet three times a week at each other's lodgings, where we drink tea, hear the chat of the day, invent fashions for the ladies, make models of 'em, and cut out patterns in paper. We were the first inventors of knotting, and this fringe is the original produce and joint labour of our little community.

Bid. And who are your pretty set, pray?

Frib. There's Phil. Whiffle, Jacky Wagtail, my lord Trip, Billy Dimple, sir Dilbery Diddle, and your humble—

Bid. What a sweet collection of happy creatures!

Frib. Indeed, and so we are, miss—But a prodigious fracas disconcerted us some time ago at Billy Dimple's—Three drunken naughty women of the town burst into our club-room, curst us all, threw down the china, broke six looking-glasses, scaled us with the slop-basin, and scratched poor Phil. Whiffle's cheek in such a manner, that he has kept his bed these three weeks.

Bid. Indeed, Mr. Fribble, I think all our sex have

great reason to be angry; for if you are so happy now you are bachelors, the ladies may wish and sigh to very little purpose.

Frib. You are mistaken, I assure you; I am prodigiously rallied about my passion for you, I can tell you that, and am looked upon as lost to our society already; he, he, he!

Bid. Pray, Mr. Fribble, now you have gone so far, don't think me imprudent if I long to know how you intend to use the lady who has been honoured with your affections?

Frib. Not as most other wives are used, I assure you; all the domestic business will be taken off her hands; I shall make the tea, comb the dogs, and dress the children myself; so that, though I'm a commoner, Mrs. Fribble will lead the life of a woman of quality; for she will have nothing to do, but lie in bed, play at cards, and scold the servants.

Bid. What a happy creature she must be!

Frib. Do you really think so? Then pray let me have a little serous talk with you—Though my passion is not of a long standing, I hope the sincerity of my intentions—

Bid. Ha, ha, ha!

Frib. Go, you wild thing! (*pats her*) The devil take me, but there is no talking to you—How can you use me in this barbarous manner? If I had the constitution of an alderman, it would sink under my sufferings—hooman nater can't support it.

Bid. Why, what would you do with me, Mr. Fribble?

Frib. Well, I vow I'll beat you if you talk so—Don't look at me in that manner——Flesh and blood can't bear it—I could—but I won't grow indecent—

Bid. But pray, sir, where are the verses you were to write upon me? I find if a young lady depends

SCENE I.   MISS IN HER TEENS.   23

too much upon such fine gentlemen as you, she'll certainly be disappointed.

Frib. I vow, the flutter I was put into this afternoon has quite turned my senses—here they are though—and I believe you'll like 'em

Bid. There can be no doubt of it.   (*courtesies.*

Frib. I protest, miss, I don't like that courtesy—Look at me, and always rise in this manner. (*rises.* But, my dear creeter, who put on your cap to-day? They have made a fright of you, and it is as yellow as old lady Crowfoot's neck.—When we are settled, I'll dress your head myself.

Bid. Pray read the verses to me, Mr. Fribble.

Frib. I obey—Hem;—William Fribble, esq. to miss Biddy Bellair——greeting.

> No ice so hard, so cold as I,
> 'Till warm'd and soften'd by your eye;
> And now my heart dissolves away
> In dreams by night, in sighs by day;
> No brutal passion fires my breast,
> Which loathes the object when possess'd;
> But one of harmless, gentle kind,
> Whose joys are center'd—in the mind;
> Then take with me love's better part,
> His downy wing, but not his dart.

How do you like 'em?

Bid. Ha, ha, ha! I swear they are very pretty—but I don't understand 'em.

Frib. These light pieces are never so well understood in reading as singing; I have set 'em myself, and will endeavour to give 'em you—La—la—I have an abominable cold, and can't sing a note; however the tune's nothing; the manner's all.   (*sings.*

No ice so hard, &c.

Enter Tag, running.

Tag. Your aunt, your aunt, your aunt, madam!

Frib. What's the matter?

H

Bid. Hide, hide Mr. Fribble, Tag, or we are ruined.

Frib. Oh! for heaven's sake, put me any where, so I don't dirty my clothes.

Bid. Put him into the store-room, Tag, this moment.

Frib. Is it a damp place, Mrs. Tag? The floor is boarded I hope?

Tag. Indeed it is not, sir.

Frib. What shall I do? I shall certainly catch my death! Where's my cambric handkerchief, and my salts? I shall certainly have my hysterics!
(runs in.

Bid. In, in, in—So, now let the other come as soon as he will; I did not care if I had twenty of 'em, so they would but come one after another.

Re-enter Tag.

Was my aunt coming?

Tag. No 'twas Mr. Flash, I suppose, by the length of his stride, and the cock of his hat. He'll be here this minute—What shall we do with him?

Bid. I'll manage him, I warrant you, and try his courage; be sure you are ready to second me—we shall have pure sport.

Tag. Hush! here he comes.

Enter Flash, singing.

Flash. Well, my blossom, here am I! What hopes for a poor dog, eh? How! the maid here! then I've lost the town, dammee! Not a shilling to bribe the governor; she'll spring a mine, and I shall be blown to the devil.

Bid. Don't be ashamed, Mr. Flash; I have told Tag the whole affair, and she's my friend, I can assure you.

Flash. Is she? then she won't be mine, I am certain. *(aside)* Well, Mrs. Tag; you know, I suppose,

SCENE I. MISS IN HER TEENS. 25

what's to be done: this young lady and I have contracted ourselves; and so, if you please to stand bridemaid, why we'll fix the wedding day directly.

Tag. The wedding-day, sir?

Flash. The wedding-day, sir? Ay, sir, the wedding-day, sir; what have you to say to that, sir?

Bid. My dear captain Flash, don't make such a noise, you'll wake my aunt.

Flash. And suppose I did, child, what then?

Bid. She'd be frightened out of her wits.

Flash. At me, miss! frightened at me? Tout au contraire, I assure you; you mistake the thing, child; I have some reason to believe I am not quite so shocking. *(affectedly.*

Tag. Indeed, sir, you flatter yourself: but pray, sir, what are your pretensions?

Flash. The lady's promises, my own passion, and the best mounted blade in the three kingdoms. If any man can produce a better title, let him take her; if not, the d——l mince me, if I give up an atom of her.

Bid. He's in a fine passion, if he would but hold it.
(aside.

Tag. Pray, sir, hear reason a little.

Flash. I never do, madam; it is not my method of proceeding; here is my logic! *(draws his sword)* Sa, sa——my best argument is cart over arm, madam, ha, ha; *(lunges)* and if he answers that, madam, through my small guts, my breath, blood, and mistress are all at his service.——Nothing more, madam.

Bid. This'll do, this'll do.

Tag. But, sir, sir, sir!

Flash. But, madam, madam, madam! I profess blood, madam; I was bred up to it from a child; I study the book of fate, and the camp is my university; I have attended the lectures of prince Charles upon the Rhine, and Bathiani upon the Po, and have extracted knowledge from the mouth of a cannon; I'm not to be frightened with squibs, madam, no, no.

Bid. Pray, dear sir, don't mind her; but let me prevail with you to go away this time—Your passion is very fine, to be sure; and when my aunt and Tag are out of the way, I'll let you know when I'd have you come again.

Flash. When you'd have me come again, child? And suppose I never would come again, what do you think of that now, ha? You pretend to be afraid of your aunt; your aunt knows what's what too well to refuse a good match when 'tis offered— Lookye, miss, I am a man of honour; glory is my aim; I have told you the road I am in; and do you see here child, (*showing his sword*) no tricks upon travellers.

Bid. But pray, sir, hear me.

Flash. No, no, no; I know the world, madam: I am as well known at Covent garden, as the dial, madam; I'll break a lamp, bully a constable, bam a justice, or bilk a box-keeper, with any man in the liberties of Westminster. What do you think of me now madam?

Bid. Pray don't be so furious, sir.

Flash. Come, come, come, few words are best; somebody's happier than somebody, and I am a poor, silly fellow; ha, ha!—That's all—Look you, child, to be short (for I'm a man of reflection) I have but a bagatelle to say to you: I am in love with you up to hell and desperation; may the sky crush me if I am not.—But since there is another more fortunate than I, adieu, Biddy! Prosperity to the happy rival, patience to poor Flash; but the first time we meet—gunpowder be my perdition, but I'll have the honour to cut a throat with him.

Bid. (*stopping him*) You may meet with him now, if you please.

Flash. Now, may I?—Where is he? I'll sacrifice the villain! (*aloud.*

Tag. Hush! he's but in the next room.

Flash. Is he? Ram me (*low*) into a mortar-piece, but I'll have vengeance; my blood boils to be at him—Don't be frightened, miss!

Bid. No, sir, I never was better pleased, I assure you.

Flash. I shall soon do his business.

Bid. As soon as you please; take your own time.

Tag. I'll fetch the gentleman to you immediately.
(*going.*

Flash. (*stopping her*) Stay, stay a little; what a passion I am in!—Are you sure he is in the next room?—I shall certainly tear him to pieces—I would fain murder him like a gentleman, too—Besides, this family shan't be brought into trouble upon my account.—I have it—I'll watch for him in the street, and mix his blood with the puddle of the next kennel. (*going.*

Bid. (*stopping him*) No, pray, Mr. Flash, let me see the battle; I shall be glad to see you fight for me; you shan't go, indeed. (*holding him.*

Tag. (*holding him*) Oh, pray let me see you fight; there were two gentlemen fit yesterday, and my mistress was never so diverted in her life—I'll fetch him out. [*exit.*

Bid. Do, stick him, stick him, captain Flash; I shall love you the better for it.

Flash. D—n your love; I wish I was out of the house. (*aside.*

Bid. Here he is—Now speak some of your hard words, and run him through—

Flash. Don't be in fits now.   (*aside to Biddy.*

Bid. Never fear me.

Enter Tag and Fribble.

Tag. (*to Fribble*) Take it on my word, sir, he is a bully, and nothing else.

Frib. (*frightened*) I know you are my good friend; but perhaps you don't know his disposition.

Tag. I am confident he is a coward.

Frib. Is he? Nay, then I'm his man.

Flash. I like his looks; but I'll not venture too far at first.

Tag. Speak to him, sir.

Frib. I will—I understand, sir—hem—that you—by Mrs. Tag here—sir—who has informed me—hem—that you would be glad to speak with me—Demme!   (*turns off.*

Flash. I can speak to you, sir—or to any body, sir—or I can let it alone, and hold my tongue—if I see occasion, sir, dammee!   (*turns off.*

Bid. Well said, Mr. Flash, be in a passion.

Tag. (*to Fribble*) Don't mind his looks; he changes colour already; to him, to him.   (*pushes him.*

Frib. Don't hurry me, Mrs. Tag, for heaven's sake! I shall be out of breath before I begin, if you do.—Sir—(*to Flash*) if you can't speak to a gentleman in another manner, sir, why then I'll venture to say, you had better hold your tongue—Oons!

Flash. Sir, you and I are of different opinions.

Frib. You and your opinion may go to the devil —Take that.   (*turns off to Tag.*

Tag. Well said, sir, the day's your own.

Bid. What's the matter, Mr. Flash? Is all your fury gone? Do you give me up?

Frib. I have done his business.   (*struts about.*

SCENE I.   MISS IN HER TEENS.   29

Flash. Give you up, madam? No, madam, when I am determined in my resolutions I am always calm: 'tis our way, madam; and now I shall proceed to business—Sir, I beg to say a word to you in private.

Frib. Keep your distance, fellow, and I'll answer you—That lady has confessed a passion for me; and as she has delivered up her heart into my keeping, nothing but my 'art's blood shall purchase it. Damnation!

Tag. Bravo! bravo!

Flash. If those are the conditions, I'll give you earnest for it directly. *(draws)* Now, villain, renounce all right and title this minute, or the torrent of my rage will overflow my reason, and I shall annihilate the nothingness of your soul and body in an instant.

Frib. I wish there was a constable at hand to take us both up; we shall certainly do one another a prejudice.

Tag. No, you won't indeed, sir; pray bear up to him; if you would but draw your sword, and be in a passion, he would run away directly.

Frib. Will he? *(draws his sword)* Then I can no longer contain myself—Hell and the furies! Come on, thou savage brute!

Tag. Go on, sir!

(*here they stand in fighting postures, while Biddy and Tag push them forward.*)

Flash. Come on.
Bid. Go on.
Frib. Come on, rascal.
Tag. Go on, sir.

        Enter Captain Loveit and Puff.

Capt. L. What's the matter, my dear?
Bid. If you won't fight, here's one that will. Oh.

Rhodophil, these two sparks are your rivals, and have pestered me these two months with their addresses; they forced themselves into the house, and have been quarrelling about me, and disturbing the family; if they won't fight, pray kick them out of the house.

Capt. L. What's the matter gentlemen?

(they both keep their fencing posture.

Flash. Don't part us, sir.

Frib. No, pray, sir, don't part us; we shall do you a mischief.

Capt. L. Puff, look to the other gentleman, and call a surgeon.

Bid. & Tag. Ha, ha, ha!

Pu. Bless me! how can you stand under your wounds, sir?

Frib. Am I hurt, sir?

Pu. Hurt, sir! why you have—let me see—pray stand in the light—one, two, three, through the heart; and let me see—hum—eight through the small guts! Come, sir, make it up the round dozen, and then we'll part you.

All. Ha, ha, ha!

Capt. L. Come here, Puff.

(whispers and looks at Flash.

Pu. 'Tis the very same, sir.

Capt. L. (to Flash) Pray, sir, have I not had the pleasure of seeing you abroad?

Flash. I have served abroad.

Capt. L. Had not you the misfortune, sir, to be missing at the last engagement in Flanders?

Flash. I was found among the dead in the field of battle.

Pu. He was the first that fell, sir; the wind of a cannon-ball struck him flat upon his face; he had just strength enough to creep into a ditch, and there he was found after the battle in a most deplorable condition.

Capt. L. Pray, sir, what advancement did you get by the service of that day?

Flash. My wounds rendered me unfit for service, and I sold out.

Pu. Stole out, you mean.—We hunted him by scent to the water-side; thence he took shipping for England; and, taking the advantage of my master's absence, has attacked the citadel, which we are luckily come to relieve, and drive his honour into the ditch again.

All. Ha, ha, ha!

Frib. He, he, he!

Capt. L. And now, sir, how have you dared to show your face in open day, or wear even the outside of a profession you have so much scandalized by your behaviour? I honour the name of a soldier, and as a party concerned am bound not to see it disgraced. As you have forfeited your title to honour, deliver up your sword this instant.

Flash. Nay, good captain—

Capt. L. No words, sir.   (*takes his sword.*)

Frib. He's a sad scoundrel! I wish I had kicked him.

Capt. L. The next thing I command——leave this house, change the colour of your clothes and fierceness of your looks; appear from top to toe the wretch, the very wretch, thou art:—If ever I meet thee in the military dress again, or if you put on looks that belie the native baseness of thy heart, be it where it will, this shall be the reward of thy impudence and disobedience. (*kicks him; he runs off.*)

Bid. Oh, my Rhodophil!

Frib. What an infamous rascal it is! I thank you, sir, for this favour; but I must after and cane him.
               (*going, he is stopped by the Captain.*

Capt. L. One word with you too, sir.

Frib. With me, sir!

Capt. L. You need not tremble; I won't use you roughly.

Frib. I am certain of that, sir; but I am sadly troubled with weak nerves.

Capt. L. Thou art of a species too despicable for correction; therefore, be gone; and if I see you here again, your insignificancy shan't protect you.

Frib. I am obliged to you for your kindness; well, if ever I have any thing to do with intrigues again!—
[*exit.*

All. Ha, ha, ha!

Pu. Shall I ease you of your trophy, sir?

Capt. L. Take it, Puff, as a small recompense for thy fidelity; thou canst better use it than its owner.

Pu. I wish your honour had a patent to take such trifles from every pretty gentleman that could spare 'em; I would set up the largest cutler's shop in the kingdom.

Capt. L. Well said, Puff.

Bid. But pray, Mr. Fox, how did you get out of your hole? I thought you was locked in.

Capt. L. I shot the bolt back when I heard a noise; and, thinking you was in danger, I broke my confinement without any other consideration than your safety. (*kisses her hand.*

Bid. I'm afraid the town will be ill-natured enough to think I have been a little coquettish in my behaviour; but I hope, as I have been constant to the captain, I shall be excused diverting myself with pretenders.

Ladies, to fops and braggarts ne'er be kind,
No charms can warm 'em and no virtues bind;
Each lover's merit by his conduct prove,
Who fails in honour, will be false in love.
[*exeunt.*

PROLOGUE.

WRITTEN BY A FRIEND.

Too long has farce, neglecting nature's laws,
Debas'd the stage, and wrong'd the comic cause;
To raise a laugh has been her sole pretence,
Though dearly purchas'd at the price of sense;
This child of folly gain'd increase of time;
Fit for the place, succeeded *pantomime*;
Reviv'd her honours, join'd her motley band,
And song and low conceit o'er-run the land.
    More gen'rous views inform our author's breast,
From real life his characters are drest;
He seeks to trace the passions of mankind,
And, while he spares the person, paints the mind.
In pleasing contrast, he attempts to show
The vap'ring bully and the fribbling beau,
Cowards alike, that full of martial airs,
And this as tender as the silk he wears.
Proud to divert, not anxious for renown,
Oft has the bard essay'd to please the town;
Your full applause out-paid his little art,
He boasts no merit but a grateful heart;
Pronounce your doom, he'll patiently submit,
Ye sov'reign judges of all works of wit!
To you the ore is brought, a lifeless mass,
You give the stamp, and then the coin may pass.
    Now, whether judgment prompt you to forgive,
Whether you bid this trifling offspring live,
Or with a frown shall send the sickly thing
To sleep whole ages under dulness' wing;
To your known candour we will always trust,
You never were, nor can you be, unjust.

EPILOGUE.

BY THE SAME FRIEND.

Good folks, I'm come at my young lady's bidding,
To say, you all are welcome to her wedding.
Th' exchange she made, what mortal here can blame?
Show me the maid that would not do the same.
For sure, the greatest monster ever seen,
Is doating *sixty* coupled to *sixteen!*
When wint'ry age had almost caught the fair,
Youth, clad in sunshine, snatch'd her from despair;
Like a new *Semele* the virgin lay,
And clasp'd her lover in the blaze of day.
Thus may each maid, the toils almost entrapp'd in,
Change *old Sir Simon* for the *brisk young Captain*.
  I love these men of arms; they know their trade:
Let dastards sue, the sons of fire invade!
They cannot bear around the bait to nibble,
Like pretty, powder'd, patient, Mr. *Fribble:*
To danger bred, and skillful in command,
They storm the strongest fortress, sword in hand!
Nights without sleep, and floods of tears when waking,
Show'd poor miss *Biddy* was in piteous taking;
She's now quite well, for maids in that condition
Find the young lover is the best physician;
And without helps of art or books of knowledge,
They cure more women, faith, than all the college!
But to the point——I come, with low petition,
For, faith, poor *Bayes* is in a sad condition;
The *huge, tall hangman** stands to give the blow,
And only waits your pleasures—Ay, or no.
If you should—*pit, box,* and *gallery,* 'egad,
Joy turns his senses, and the man runs mad!
But if your ears are shut, your hearts are rock,
And you pronounce the sentence—Block to block,
Down kneels the bard, and leaves you, when he's dead,
The empty tribute of an author's head.

    * Alluding to *Bayes'* prologue in the *Rehearsal*.

HERO AND LEANDER.

A Comic Burletta,

IN TWO ACTS.

BY ISAAC JACKMAN.

CORRECTLY GIVEN,

AS PERFORMED AT THE THEATRES ROYAL.

With Remarks.

NEW-YORK:
Published by CHARLES WILEY, No. 3, Wall-street,
And H. C. CAREY & I. LEA, and M'CARTY & DAVIS,
Philadelphia.

1824.

G. F. Hopkins, printer, 48 Pine-street.

REMARKS.

This Burletta, remarkable principally for the occasion which produced it, was written by Isaac Jackman for Mr. John Palmer, who had then recently built and opened the Royalty Theatre, in Well-street, Goodman's-fields, for the regular drama. Continued opposition from the patentees of the royal theatres obliged that gentleman to renounce his first intention, and this elegant Theatre (though better calculated, in every respect, for the *legitimate* drama than the winter theatres) has been, since that period, opened under an annual license for burletta, pantomime, &c. according to the Act 25th Geo. II.

In his dedication, the author observes, that " the worthy manager requested me to write something for him *within the statute*, and I thought poor Hero and Leander might be introduced to the public, without being considered ' *wagrants* or *wagabones!*' I did intend to souse Leander in the waves, as a part of the old romance, and to have a requiem sung over his manes; but a wicked wit told me, that such a denouement would be *tragedy* direct, and against the law."

At the first representation of this afterpiece, the talents of Mr. Bannister, Mr. W. Palmer, Mr. Arrowsmith, Mrs. Fox, Master Braham, &c. ensured it the highest success.

During the controversy elicited by Mr. Palmer's endeavours to obtain a patent for his theatre, it was aptly observed, that " it is of no consequence to government, or to the million residing within the walls of London, whether the winter managers and Mr. Coleman play to empty benches or overflowing audiences. If they are able, diligent, and liberal, they cannot fail of accumulating very considerable fortunes, and may bid defiance to every exertion of Mr. Palmer in the east: let this be as it may, the public good ought first to be consulted."

An unjust and impolitic monopoly, however, preserved the ascendency; and the public good, as on many other more important occasions, was sacrificed to private interests.

DRAMATIS PERSONÆ.

                                  Royal Theatre, 1787.
Abudah .... Mr. *W. Palmer.*
Delah .... Mr. *Chambers.*
Leander .... Mr. *Arrowsmith.*
Hymen .... Master *Braham.*
Solano .... Mr. *Bannister.*
    Soldiers, Labouring People, Men and Women.
Hero .... Mrs. *Fox.*
Safrina .... Mrs. *Burnet.*
Minerva .... Miss *Burnet.*

SCENE—The Banks of the Hellespont. Time—Sun-rise.

HERO AND LEANDER.

ACT THE FIRST.

SCENE I. A HARVEST SCENE, AT SUN-RISE, ON THE BANKS OF THE HELLESPONT.

Turkish husbandmen at work, their wives employed at the same time.—A perspective view of the castle of Abydos, in Natolia or the Lesser Asia—the Hellespont appearing to divide the two countries.

Enter Solano, Safrina, Hero, labouring men and women.

Chorus. ALL hail the cheerful god of day,
Parent of ev'ry human bliss;
Who (ere he wings his heav'nly way)
Salutes his Thetis with a kiss.
Safrina. See how creation smiles around;
What melody enchants the grove!
Hero. 'Tis there the voice of nature's found
Responsive to the note of love.
Chorus. All hail, &c.

Sol. Well done, my lads, the morning seems to low'r;
In yonder clouds, methinks, I view a show'r;
Bind up the corn, harness all the cattle,
And let the women quit their idle prattle;
Those lazy sluts are constantly a gadding;
'Tis such as you, that set the fellows madding.

Hero. Behold Aurora, with a blushing ray
And rosy fingers, spreads the infant day!

Song—Hero.

Ere yet Aurora chase the dews,
The lark his matin song renews;
And seems to chide the swain's delay,
To lose so sweet a part of day.

See from the ground his mate arise,
And seems to mock our wond'ring eyes;
Still as she soars her notes decay,
Till the faint warblings die away.

Sol. Well, Safrina, what's the mattter now?
Saf. There sits, alas, on gentle Hero's brow
A settled grief.
Sol. Psha! I know the reason:
Hero's nineteen, and that, you know,'s the season
When females would be married, if they could.
Saf. Well, what of that? are we not flesh and
    blood?

Song—Safrina.

When I was young, I danc'd and sung,
My heart was lighter than a fly;
No care my youthful bosom stung,
At ev'ry rout, pray who but I?

At length the urchin bent his bow,
The vagrant arrow hit the mark;
But Hymen, 'solv'd his skill to show,
Cur'd poor Safrina in the dark.

Sol. Well done, Safrina; foregad, we all can tell,
There was a time, you bore away the belle.

(*a peal of thunder; sky appears overcast: exeunt Safrina and Hero.*)

Sol. Away, my lads—the storm is drawing near
And save the produce of a fruitful year.

(*a peal of thunder, accompanied with lightning.*)

SCENE I.   HERO AND LEANDER.   9

Sol. Well done, my boys! The clouds are all on
    fire;
A thunderbolt hath struck the village spire.
            (a peal of thunder, lightning, rain, &c.
  Sol. The hills are wrapt in stormy clouds on high,
And feel the dread convulsion of the sky;
Tempests arise, on fortune's ocean low'r,
And rolling billows lash th' affrighted shore.
(tempest rages; a man, standing on a rock, cries out—
  Man. A ship, a ship! 'twixt sea and wind she
    strives.
  Sol. Fly all, fly all, and save the people's lives.

      Song—*Solano.*

Alas, how chang'd the face of things; *(thunder and*
Hark, hark, the howling tempest sings: *lightning.*
Ah, now the rebel winds she feels,
Toss'd on the billows, how she reels!

She's now a wreck, behold on high   *(thunders.*
Exploded thunder rends the sky;
A dread convulsion moves the shore,
And rocks the deep unmov'd before.

The crew now appear landing—thunder and light-
ning—music descriptive of the elemental warfare
—Storm gradually decreases—Leander disguised.

  Sol. Welcome on shore, sir, whether friend or foe,
All are our brothers in this scene of wo.
  Lean. Thanks to you, gentle friends; and, sir, to
    you,
Our constant prayers are ever, ever due;
May all the powers divine your labours bless,
And send you friends, if ever in distress!
  Sol. What means that sigh? ah tell me, gentle
    youth;
You seem the child of honour and of truth:
Banish your cares, for see, the God of light
Dispels the gloom, that wrapp'd the world in night.

Lean. Stern Boreas, frowning, now forsakes the plain,
And smiling Nature visits us again;
Each tree its wonted foliage re-assumes,
And new-born zephyrs breathe around perfumes.
Where'er we turn to view our ravish'd eyes,
Luxuriant scenes of endless beauty rise.

Song—Leander.

> Transparent now, and all serene,
>   The gentle current flows;
> While fancy draws the flatt'ring scene,
>   How fair the landscape shows!
>
> But soon its transient charms decay,
>   When ruffling tempests blow;
> The soft delusions fleet away,
>   And pleasure ends in wo.

Sol. Tell me, gentle sir, from whence you came;
Declare your sovereign, country, and your name;
Are ye from Natolia's rebel coast?
If that be so, 'twere better you were lost.
                            (trumpet without.
The chief is rous'd: behold him, great in arms;
Let Hero now subdue him with her charms:
From yonder mountain's brow he saw your sails;
Dreadful he is—a bashaw of three tails.
   (music plays—'see the conquering hero comes.'
Enter Abudah on an elephant, attended with a numerous body of guards, armed with spears.

Abu. What's this I see?—a set of rascal minions
Hanging together, like a bunch of onions.
I'll hang ye all, aye, scoundrels, before night,
If on the instant you don't quit my sight.

Sol. Dread sir, we have got some prisoners here,
That seem half dead already with their fear;
Shipwreck'd upon our coast, we sav'd their lives,
And here they are——

SCENE I. HERO AND LEANDER. 11

 Abu. Say, have they any wives?
The women all are mine—yes, if twenty,
Although indeed I've petticoats in plenty.
 Sol. We found no female, sir, among the crew;
Shall we discharge the men—pray what say you?
 Abu. Let them all breakfast, ⎫
Each a loaf of bread,   ⎬ *prisoners bow.*
And then let ev'ry prisoner— ⎪
Lose his head.   ⎭

Chorus.—Prisoners.

  Have pity, great Chief,
  And send us relief:
  We're all in a wretched condition:
  O, spare our poor lives,
  And we'll send you our wives—
  Accept this our humble petition.

during this chorus Abudah alights.

 Abu. Silence, rascals!—I find you then can prate,
But, scoundrels, you shall know my word is fate.
My sword shall treat the vultures with a feast;
Shall lay whole realms, nay, human nature, waste.
 Sol. I told them, sir, how great you were in pow'r,
That with a single puff you'd rock a tow'r;
That you were ten feet high—was not that right?
 Abu. Ten feet at least—five cubits—No—not quite:
Yet ev'ry inch is made of proper stuff,
Tho' idle nature cast me in the rough.

Song.—Abudah.

  Stand all aloof, ye paltry jades,
  And you, ye filthy knaves of spades;
  How dare you look beyond those pales,
  On me, who wear three thumping tails?
  Don't you all know, that at a blow,
  I'd send you to the shades below?
  Begone, or else I swear odsbobs,
  I'll send you home without your knobs.

Enter—Hero.

But Hero now her form displays,
And strives to charm a thousand ways;
From head to foot new modes of dress,
Her various arts to please express:
I find I'm caught within the snare,
So I'll enjoy the am'rous fair;
As I'm a soldier great and stout,
This girl has turn'd me inside out.

(*Hero and Leander look steadfastly at each other.*
Lean. It is, it is my love! Ye gods be kind!
(*aside.*
Hero. 'Tis he—I give my sorrows to the wind. (*aside.*
Abu. What does the fellow stare at? Speak, you
  dog.
The rascal seems as stupid as a log.
  Lean. Spare your reproaches, sir; I'm ill at ease,
My life is yours, do with me as you please.
See tear succeeds to tear—a passage seeks, (*aside.*
And, bursting forth, bedews her lovely cheeks.
  Abu. No grumbling, sirrah. Charmer, let's retire,
           (*takes Hero by the hand.*
The god of love shall fan the keen desire;
My body, blood, and soul are all on fire.   (*going.*
  Lean. Monster, avaunt!——Release the heavenly
      fair,
Or, by all the avenging powers, I swear——
           (*seizes Abudah.*
  Abu. Seize, seize the villain; drag him to the
      block,
Or toss him headlong from the steepest rock.
No, off with his head.   As I'm a sinner,
I'll have his knob, before I eat my dinner.
  Hero. Mercy, O mercy, sir, as you are great!
O save the youth, at least suspend his fate!
  Abu. Who is the vagabond?
  Lean. Why, caitiff, hear,
So shall thy savage nature shake with fear;

Know then, ingrate, from Abydos I came;
Still more; know thou, Leander is my name.
(throws off his disguise.
Now slip thy bloodhounds—'dulge the savage rout;
I stand unmov'd.
 Abu. O now the murder's out.
Thanks to thee, prophet, thanks to thee again.
—Speak not in his behalf, you sue in vain;
This is the squire, that braves the Hellespont,
And steals at night to madam hot-upon't.
Zounds! I'll souse him in a tub of pickle;
And as to miss, her toby I will tickle.
Drag him away.

Hero. Great chief, be not cruel, but good as you're brave,
  Remember, the hero but conquers to save.
Sol. Give life to the wretched, whose fate's in your hand,
  'Tis humanity graces and blesses the land.
Lean. I sue not for mercy, I stand here unmov'd,
  Protected by virtue, by beauty, and love.
All. Look down, O ye gods, and let mortals now prove,
  The blessings that wait upon virtue and love.

 Hero. Hear me, great sir—O spare Leander's life,
Grant this request, and Hero is your wife.
 Sol. Say, will your actions with your words accord?
 Hero. They will indeed.
 Sol. Then take her at her word.
 Lean. I read my Hero's meaning in her eyes.
(aside.
 Abu. It is all flummery.—By heaven, he dies.
 Hero. Pardon me, sir, my love for you prevails,
What girl can stand a bashaw of three tails?
(coaxes him.

Song—Hero.

O, sir, be consenting, be kind and relenting,
Release these poor creatures, and send them away;
 Do but this, and you'll find
 How good-natur'd and kind
I'll prove to my spousee, by night, and by day.

O, come now, sweet lover, a passion discover,
  A sly little Cupid now lurks in that smile;
    Ev'ry maid must surrender
    To such a commander,
  You've found out a way my poor heart to beguile.
Behold, like Apollo, his ringlets of yellow!
  Behold how, like Mars, at this moment he stands!
    His breath too discloses
    The perfume of roses!
How plump his round cheeks, and how taper his hands.
  O, come now, sweet lover, &c.

Abu. A pretty soul it is!—Say will you, miss,
Give your bashaw the earnest of a kiss.
                    (kisses him.
'Tis done! 'tis done!—you're pardon'd, rascals go,
I give you life, my love will have it so.
But if that poaching dog comes here again,
And braves my anger, as he braves the main,
I'll whip the rebel rascal, till he's blind.—
Be scarce then, scoundrels, now you know my mind.

Chorus—Prisoners.

Happy, happy, happy day;
Ev'ry heart its homage pay.

Chorus—by the Turks.

Wake to harmony the voice,
Rejoice, 'tis mercy calls, rejoice.

(during this chorus, Abudah mounts the elephant; he first places his foot on the shoulder of a slave, who kneels and raises him gently, until Abudah vaults into the saddle.

Chorus—All.

Happy, happy, happy day,
Ev'ry heart its homage pay.
Wake to harmony the voice,
Rejoice, 'tis mercy calls, rejoice.

ACT THE SECOND.

SCENE I. A GROVE.

Enter Abudah, Solano, Safrina, and Hero.

Abu. Come, come, Solano, methinks we tarry,
I shall be all a-gog, until I marry.
The loves in council sit, and from above
Venus now calls me to the Paphian grove.
  Sol. What says my gentle Hero, will you go?
  Saf. Her heart seems bursting with its grief.
  Hero. Heigh ho!
  Saf. Divide your sorrows, Hero, give me part.
Suppress that sigh—or else you'll break my heart.

Song—Safrina.

Alas! I press'd, with growing love,
  This darling to my breast;
Not the most favour'd, e'en above,
  Was more completely bless'd.

Dear innocent! her lovely smiles
  Delight me but to view;
And ev'ry pang my Hero feels,
  Her mother feels it too.

  Abu. I see she's coy, yet love is in her eye,
She'll know her bashaw better by and by;
Come, Hero, I hope there's no repenting,
The gods, my pretty chicken—are consenting.

Song—Abudah.

Gentle Hero! take my hand,
Love and life's at thy command:
  Joys surrounding,
  Sorrows drowning,
Bliss shall gladden all the land.
  But if you refuse me,
  And think but to noose me
In love's silken fetters,
And sneer at your betters,
  By the gods now I swear,
  From your bosom I'll tear—

    No, stop—I'll do more,
    I'll deluge the shore
    With blood—
    Till nature looks wild,
    And before I retire,
    I'll kindle a fire,
    That shall toast you,
    And roast you,
    Man, woman, and child.

Saf. O mercy on us! whither shall we fly?
Sol. He'll ravish you, perhaps.
Saf. No, first I'll die.
   (*exeunt Safrina and Hero ; huzza without.*
    Enter Delah and Soldiers.

Abu. What's the matter, Delah?
Del. Dread sir, attend—
We've seen a sail—I'm sure she's not a friend—
Hovering on our coast; she's full of people.
I saw her first, great sir, from yonder steeple.
 Abu. Rally my forces—instant line the strand;
They're rebel rascals, from Natolia's land.
   (*exit Delah ; soldiers remain. Huzza without.*
Like Mars, I'll dart the javelin from my car,
I scorn to wait, I'll meet the coming war.
    (*going ; trumpet sounds without.*
 Sol. Fir'd by the sound, my genius bids me go,
To share the conflict, and repel the foe.

    Song—Solano.
  Hark! the trumpet sounds afar,
  The clam'rous harbinger of war;
  Rouse, soldiers, rouse, to arms, to arms,
  The call my beating bosom warms;
  The foe insults our native shore;
  And proudly mocks his conqueror.

     Air.

  O, genius of this happy land,
  Descend! and bless thy chosen band;
  Give us to meet the daring foe,
  'Tis liberty shall nerve the blow.

So when the toils of war are o'er,
And meek-ey'd peace unlocks her store;
Each youthful hero then shall prove,
A sweet reward in faithful love.

Enter Delah.

Del. Dread sir, a prisoner we have taken.
Abu. Off with his head—I'll make the fellow bacon.
Del. If you unhead him, sir, he cannot speak.
Abu. What horrid fear sits trembling on thy cheek?
Del. I find Leander, sir, comes here to-night,
To visit Hero, and secure her flight.
Abu. Death and the devil!—this is news indeed—
O for Bellona's whip to make him bleed!
He should be more than twenty months in dying,
'Twould make me smile, to see the rascal frying.
Sol. Suppose we seize him as he comes to night,
Waylay the villain—nab him?
Abu. That is right.
You counsel well, Solano—Come away,
My soul's in arms, and eager for its prey.

[exeunt omnes.

SCENE II. NIGHT.

The Hellespont in perspective. Leander is seen rowing himself over. A candle appears in Hero's window, as a direction to her lover.

Enter Abudah, Solano, and soldiers.

Sol. Behold him, sir—his fate, alas! draws nigh,
And forces e'en the tribute of a sigh.
Like the dread genius of the deep he steers,
Nor shuns the labour, nor the danger fears.

Song—Solano.

O, see how he comes, how he moves thro' the gloom,
Conducted by fate, and by love, to his doom!

O, see the fond youth, to the shore now he bends,
And quits his companions, his country, and friends;
Regardless of danger, he darts thro' the wave,
'Tis nature commands him, and nature must save.

Abu. The fellow's got on shore, he'll soon be here;
The light conducts him to my faithless fair.
O here he comes—be silent all as death,
Let not a creature speak, above his breath..
Enter Leander.

Lean. Well, so far safe—I now must wait to see
The bright perfection of a deity.
O do not, cruel love, my cares prolong!
I'll wake my gentle Hero with a song.

Song—Leander.
Awake, my sweet Hero, my heart's dearest treasure,
  Leander now calls you to love and delight;
'Tis Hymen shall sanctify love's softest pleasure,
  Give our days all to joy, and to rapture the night.
Awake then my charmer, and share the sweet blessing,
  The moments now fly me, alas! how distressing;
O, think of our joys, when caress'd and caressing,
  Arise, my sweet Hero, love calls you away.
                (*Hero opens the window.*

Hero. O my soul's joy! thy cheering voice I hear;
Like notes of seraphs, rushing on my ear.
Lean. O come, my Hero, bless again my arms,
My heart, still constant, beats with love's alarms!
Danger could work no change, nor time remove
The honest warmth of undissembled love.
Haste then, sweet fair, thy lover's transport meet,
Fly to his arms, and make his bliss complete.
                (*Hero shuts the window.*
That heaven from which no secret is conceal'd,
But ev'ry wish and thought must stand reveal'd,
Views not a love more pure, or truer mind,
Amongst the various race of human kind;
Where neither int'rest nor design have part,
But all the warmth is native from the heart.
            (*Enter Hero; Leander embraces her.*

SCENE II. HERO AND LEANDER. 19

Lean. O bless'd event!—lets fly to yonder shore:
We've met, my Hero, now, to part no more.
Hail, happy groves, retreats of peace and joy,
Where no black cares the mind's repose destroy!
　Hero. Discharg'd from care, on unfrequented plains.
We'll sing of rural joys in rural strains;
No false corrupt delights our thoughts shall move,
But joys of friendship, tenderness, and love.

Duet.

Lean. Come now, my sweet love, to the grove,
　　　The graces are waiting for you;
　　Thro' roses and woodbines we'll rove,
　　　And kiss as all true lovers do.
Hero. O, take both my hand and my heart,
　　　My lover I know he is true;
　　Till death shall direct us to part,
　　　We'll kiss as all true lovers do.
Both. Adieu then to doubt and despair,
　　　Fair virtue our loves will pursue;
　　We'll not know a moment of care,
　　　But kiss, as all true lovers do.

(*they appear retiring to Leander's vessel, but are stopt by Abudah, Solano, Delah, and soldiers; the soldiers present their spears at Leander.*

　Abu. Bind the villain.—O sir, you're caught again!
Knock off his head, and let me have his brain;
Now that my anger's rous'd, my rage is full,
I'll make a punch-bowl of the rascal's skull.

(*in this part of the scene, Minerva, in a cloud, attended by Hymen, descends in the back scene, supposed to be the banks of the Hellespont.*

　Lean. O now farewell to hope!—My love adieu,
I die content, because I die for you.
　Hero. O make his cause, ye Powers above, your care,
Let guilt shrink back, and innocence appear!

Support his soul, now death demands his prey,
And smooth his passage to the realms of day!
   Lean. May heaven still guard her with peculiar care,
And make her happy, as it made her fair!
May calmest peace her future days attend,
And late may she to endless joys ascend!
   Abu. Bring me a cauldron, hot as Alecto's kettle;
First Medusa's snaky whip shall try his mettle!
'Sdeath! his blood I'll bottle, and in the dark profound
I'll sprinkle libations to the furies round.

       (*Minerva and Hymen come forward; Abudah
       starts; all stand amazed.*

   Min. Cease, hell-hound—infernal monster, cease—
I come, the blessed harbinger of peace,
To join in Hymen's bands, this constant pair,
The youth deserving, and the virtuous fair;
Their constancy and truth deserve my care.
Stand forth, my children—Hymen, join their hands.

      (*a flourish of trumpets; they kneel and Hymen
      joins their hands.*

'Tis Wisdom consecrates the sacred bands.

       Song—Hymen.

   Sweetest pleasures never ceasing,
    Blessings, which the gods present,
   Joys with length of years increasing,
    Rosy health, and sweet content,
   Await the fair, and deck the youth,
   United in the bands of truth.

   And when old Time, with solemn pace,
    Shall call to tell them, both must die;
   Touch'd as he views their fond embrace,
    He'll bless them first, then pass them by.
    Sweetest pleasures, &c.

   Abu. What then, is all my greatness come to this?
Am I then baffled by a paltry miss?—

SCENE II.   HERO AND LEANDER.   21

Your power, madam, certainly prevails;
Wisdom, I find, pays no respect to tails.
Lean. O thanks, eternal thanks, to you be given,
Thou best and brightest ornament of Heaven!
Min. Now strike the sprightly lyre; all care away,
To mirth and joy we dedicate the day;
I'll raise an altar to love's holy flame,
Inscrib'd with Hero's and Leander's name.

Finale.

Lean.   Joy and pleasure now go round,
            Beauty's triumph is to day;
          Ev'ry voice in chorus sound,
            This is Hymen's holiday.
          Dress a garland for the fair,
            Care and sorrow hither go;
              Daffodillies,
              Virgin-lilies—
          Hymen says he'll have it so.
Hero.   Take my hand, you have my heart,
            Indeed you've had it long ago;
          And now we'll never, never, part—
            Hymen says, he'll have it so.
Chorus. Joy and pleasure, &c.
Saf.   Cupid is a foolish boy.
            Once on me he tried his bow;
          But I never felt a joy,
            Till Hymen said he'd have it so.
Chorus. Joy and pleasure, &c.
Abu.   Must I then give up the fair,
            And see them laughing at my wo
          Live and lead a life of care?
            The devil sure would have it so.
Chorus. Joy and pleasure, &c.
Sol.   Observe ye fair, the moral here—
            Let virtue in your bosoms glow;
          You then may bid adieu to fear—
            Hymen says he'll have it so.
Chorus. Joy and pleasure, &c.

THE END OF HERO AND LEANDER.

K